In

SUPPOUT!!

Be a Strong Blessing

MARCIE R. CURRY

2010

This Book Published By The Talking Bout, LLC
Front Cover Design © By Jeremiah Shephatiah

Be a Strong Blessing

Library of Congress Control Number: 2010938245

ISBN- 978-0-9802217-9-4

Printed in the United States of America

CONTENTS

FOREWORD

When you look in the dictionary for the word "driven" you will find a picture of Marcie Curry, a breath of fresh air that takes you away. A strong blessing from God that has a heart filled with love. The thing that drives her is the passion for a younger generation to become educated on breast cancer. Marcie lost her aunt to the disease and has been on a mission ever since. All of her power and strength comes from the hunger to succeed in her quest to provide information to the world. She wants to save a generation who may think this cause is not at the top of an individual to-do list. From where I am sitting, she is well on her way.

When we met, her smile melted me and our connection grew immediately after I bought a ticket to an event to celebrate breast cancer survivors and to educate those who have never lost a loved one to this disease. After attending the Pink & Black Gala, I knew my friend would reach every young woman's heart that would dare cross her path. To this day, she remains focused. It is the kind of drive that makes you desire to move and help her in every way that you can.

As humans, we take so much for granted. Marcie knows how precious life is and she will get the word out by any means necessary so that another generation will not be lost. Education is power, and in the first hand accounts you will read in these heartfelt chapters, you will find a cross section of individuals who experienced the same trauma and have bonded in a unique way; the way only God can join two or more in His Name.

God is moving in her life and mine. We do not know where the path will lead us. We are just happy to go along on the journey that God has destined for us. I know that I am blessed beyond measure to have survived this disease because so many soldiers did not. His mysteries we sometimes do not understand, but we accept His Will for our lives and say humbly - Thank You!

Marcie knows what she wants and how to go after it. Ideas dance through her head and with a determination like no other, she executes them. What a wonderful seat I have to enjoy the journey of Marcie Curry. My seat belt is fastened and take off has begun. Ms. Marcie Curry is definitely a strong blessing to so many of us who need her. Come and be a part of this voyage with us.

Judith Davis-Crenshaw

PREFACE

In 2004, I was introduced to Breast Cancer for the first time when I volunteered for the Avon Breast Cancer walk in Charlotte, North Carolina. This was the first time I ever witnessed how breast cancer had played a large part in the lives of so many men and women - being diagnosed, supporting diagnosed family or friends, the loss of a loved one, or even being a survivor. From that day forward, my passion and appreciation for the disease grew. A million and one thoughts and questions raced through my mind; such as, "How can so many people be diagnosed with this disease?" and "Where did it come from?" So I started reading to educate myself, and thinking and praying about how I could get the word out to the larger community.

Then, in 2007 my Heavenly Father blessed me with both a mission and a vision. My vision was to start a breast cancer organization that would educate people about breast cancer, treatment, and the importance of getting regular mammograms. I also wanted to start an online social community where people nationwide could communicate and provide support to one another. In

2008, I started Strong Blessings Social Connection that provides support to those who have breast cancer or have lost love ones due to the disease. According to statistics, breast cancer is the leading form of cancer in women today and is the second leading cause of cancer death in women worldwide. Breast cancer not only affects the person battling the disease, but it also affects family members, friends, co- workers and other loved ones. There is no need to wait until the loss of a loved one to educate yourself to this deadly disease. Through encouragement, education, and community support to young men and women throughout the Central Savannah River Area (CSRA) and nationwide, Strong Blessings Social Connection (SBSC) will provide you with the support you need.

Sadly to say, in 2006, my aunt was diagnosed with breast cancer, and in October 2007, we lost her to the disease. At the time, it was very hard for me and my family to deal with our loss, and it still is even after three years. However, prayer and strong faith is helping us deal with our sorrow. As someone who has suffered through the loss of a loved one from breast cancer, I am here to inform and educate you so you won't be left in the dark and asking the question "Why?" Why, is the question everyone asks when they have lost a loved one. But, that is really not our place to ask because we are not questioning ourselves, we are questioning God. We are no shape or form to question God about anything he does in our life. God put us here temporarily, and when he feels like our job is done, he will call us home. So, I'm not going to question my Heavenly Father, I will simply live up to my purpose and mission he put me on earth to accomplish. I know my aunt is shining down on me and is very proud of everything I am doing and have done to help educate people on breast cancer, especially the importance of getting regular mammograms.

Be spiritual my sisters and brothers, by being a walking conduct of God's love. Don't let trials and tribulations get you down, as it is all a part of the journey of living, loving and overcoming your battle. According to recent statistics, breast cancer is the most common cancer in the world today. Breast Cancer can occur in your 20's, but it is more likely to occur after the age of 40. As women, young or old, this is the time to start educating yourself about this disease. I am going to teach you about measures you can take to protect yourself, and ways to detect breast cancer early. When found and treated in its early stages, the chance for successful treatment is greater. A mammogram can find cancer when it's very small, often several months before you or your doctor can see it. Many younger women are unaware that they are at risk for breast cancer because there is no effective breast cancer screening for women under the age of 40. There is very little research focused on issues unique to this younger population. Young women diagnosed with breast cancer often feel isolated from peers who can relate to what they have or are experiencing.

As someone who has experienced the devastating effects of breast cancer, I set out to write this book to provide greater insight and better understanding of this disease. Along the way, I wanted to provide inspiring and motivational words for those living and dealing with the disease. As a result, I have asked several individuals to share their incredible stories about family members, friends, and co-workers who have gone through different facets of breast cancer.

Thank you to all of the strong, dedicated individuals who contributed their wonderful stories of hope and inspiration to this book.

ON A WING AND A PRAYER

I'll never forget that fateful day
When I heard the doctors say
We have bad news, the tests are in
I suddenly lost my happy grin

They said don't fret, but to no avail
We will get through this, we will not fail
There is no choice, we must stand tall
And beat this thing, once and for all

Three months have passed and I am weak
My body's tired, my soul so bleak
I will get through this, that I know
But at this moment, it does not show

I want to rest my weary fears
And pretend for a moment that I don't care
To carry them all through the day
Just makes it harder…please go away

Four months have passed and I am bright
My cheery soul shines through the night

I think I've beat this monster's grip
My strength and courage, I came equipped

Today's the day they'll tell me so
You've beat this thing…one month to go
Let's sing and dance the night away
I'm happy now…so won't you stay

I always knew right from the start
I would prevail…for I've got heart
They said don't fret…what did they know
I had to prove it was my show

I fought this beast and now I've won
Thank you mommy…said my son
I don't know what I would have done
For it was all or merely none

I've shown such strength and through it all
I never wavered, I stood so tall
I made it through, from there to here
All because of a wing and a prayer

TESTIMONIES

*Before the Storm: When I Was
First Diagnosed with
Breast Cancer*

Even though I had performed many self breast exams and received my annual physical exam, in October of 2005 my life changed forever. After my annual physical exam, I was scheduled for a normal mammogram which revealed a small abnormality in my left breast. The abnormality was one which was too small to be detected by just performing a self exam. Because of the abnormality which showed up on the mammogram, I had to receive a magnetic resonance imaging (MRI) test. I stress the importance of getting your annual mammogram.

Based on the MRI, unfortunately physicians at Medical College of Georgia Health Breast Cancer Clinic diagnosed it as Stage 1 Cancer, a type of cancer that is known to quickly spread to the unaffected breast. After consulting with physicians, family, and prayer, I decided to have a double mastectomy, which was performed by Dr. Scott Lind, M.D. an oncology surgeon with MCG Cancer Center two months later in December of 2005.

I was really overjoyed that the physicians moved fast and aggressively, because pathology reports revealed the cancer had already spread to my right breast as well. The day I was told about the diagnosis, I was never in fear. I knew and believed that God would always be with me. I did however have a little anxiety regarding the ordeal, but never an ounce of fear. My anxiety was eliminated because of the caring and supportive treatment team at MCG Cancer Clinic. While going through treatment and all the required medical attention, I was evaluated by an oncologist surgeon, medical oncologist, radiation oncologist and reconstructive surgeon, all in one day at the same location. Their consideration of my time and that of my family was overwhelming and they were able to give me and my family a clearer understanding of what was to come.

Even though a diagnosis as such would normally traumatize many, I never faltered because I knew through God I would receive a miracle. I never gave up on God nor did I stop hoping through the entire ordeal, that Divine favor would be mine. I believe God cured me the day I was diagnosed. God will do the same for you, if you only believe. I did not understand everything that was going on from the diagnosis through surgery to recovery, but the one thing I did know was that I could always trust God. At 57 years of age, FIVE years cancer free, I am here today to tell you that Divine Favor can also be yours. BELIEVE.

Starr Brown Martin

I never asked, "Why me?" It was more like, "Why now?" This wasn't supposed to be happening to me especially not now. I was 29 years old and just had my first child, a son, 5 months ago, and I was enjoying being a new mom. I wanted to do everything right for my baby which included breast feeding. I did for about 8 weeks. Before I stopped breast feeding, I noticed a large lump that would not go away. It was about the size of a small orange! I thought it was breast milk so I ignored it for about two months. It never crossed my mind that it (the lump) was cancer. After all, I was still young, but I knew I have a family history of breast cancer, so after discussing my newly found lump with concerned family and friends, I decided to go to the doctor. I thought that maybe my breasts were engorged or it was just some type o f breast infection from breast feeding. I went to the doctor and once he became aware of my family history, he immediately set up an appointment for a mammogram.

Here it is, Monday morning, October 1, 2007, the first day of National Breast Cancer Awareness Month and here I am sitting in a doctor's office waiting to have my first mammogram. I had a mammogram and an ultrasound as well. They thanked me for coming in to get a mammogram and gave me a breast cancer awareness goodie bag. I left and went to work. I wasn't even at work for two hours before my doctor's office called and asked me to come in immediately, today to have a biopsy. I said, "Ok." Again, it never crossed my mind that this could be bad. For the second time in a day, I was on my way to another doctor's office. I got the biopsy done and the doctor told me to call back the next day after 3 o'clock for my results. I called the next day, and I was told that I need to have another mammogram done but they didn't say why and I didn't ask. I went back to the doctor a few days later and the doctor told me that it "looks" like cancer, that's what he believes it is, and I need to have another biopsy done to be sure. Even after hearing all that I still didn't think that this was going to be bad. I refused to believe that something like this (cancer) could be happening to me, especially now! By this time I knew the routine—call back the next day after 3 o'clock for the results.

The next day at work I was nervous the whole day. I remember watching the clock and waiting for 3 o'clock. When the time finally came, I couldn't even pick up the phone. I decided I would wait a few more minutes. Before I knew it, it was almost 4 o'clock. It was now time for me to make the biggest phone call of my life! I called my doctor's office—I told the nurse I was calling for my biopsy results she said, "Ok" and asked me to hold. I was on hold for what felt like a lifetime. I was trying to remain calm and relaxed as I listened to the music playing in the background. I couldn't help but wonder why it was taking so long for the nurse to come back to the phone. I thought to myself, "Well, if it is bad (cancer) the doctor will be the one to give me the results, not the nurse. Then again, maybe they're just busy?" I continued to hold and sing along with the 80's tune that was playing—*Every Breath You Take* by Sting & The Police. Finally, someone came back to the phone. The next voice I heard was the voice of my doctor...I knew it was bad! My doctor gave me the news in such a tactful manner that I didn't even have time to react and let the news that I have cancer sink in. All I remember after that is the doctor saying that he wanted to meet with me and my family to talk about my options. All I could do was think about how I was going to get out of here (work), without being seen and go pick up my son from daycare without falling apart. I asked God, "Please give me the strength that I need to get out of here and get home!"

I left work, picked up my son and went home. I walked in the house and put my son down in his playpen. My sister asked," Did you hear from the doctor yet?" I had my back to her—I shook my head yes. "What did he say?" she asked. Still, with my back to her I just looked down at my son and shook my head no. I just wanted to scream and holler but my two nephews and my son were right there and I did not want to scare them. I quickly left the room and my sister followed. I burst into tears! I cried out, "He (doctor) said its cancer!" I remember my sister holding me in her arms as I cried and telling me that it was going to be ok. Once I got myself together, she told me to call Mom. I didn't know how I was going to break the news to her. I called my mother and told her that I—her baby girl, had breast cancer. I don't remember her initial reaction I think she said, "Oh no!" But I just remember her talking to me with a calm, soft voice, "Everything is going to be alright—Mama is praying for you and I'm going to be here for you every step of the way. I survived (breast cancer) and you will too! If your faith is as strong as I think it is you are going to be just fine." I felt so much better after talking to her after all; she's the strongest woman I know. If she survived breast cancer, I knew I could too.

Telling everyone that I had breast cancer was the most difficult thing I have ever had to do! I didn't sleep very well that night because all I could think about was how I was going to tell the rest of my family—my father , my great-grandmother, my boyfriend and my closest friends that I have breast cancer. The next morning (Thursday) I had to call my job to tell them that I had cancer and I would not be in for the rest of the week. My hands were shaking and I was starting to cry. I only wanted one of two people to answer the phone because they both have such great spirits and they always have the right words to say. I didn't want to talk to anyone else— unless I had to. "Please God, let one of them answer the phone!" She answered the phone. "Thank you Jesus!" I said to myself. The first thing she said to me was," Did you get your results yet?" I said, "Yes." She said, "Well?" I paused for a moment then I said, "Its cancer!" I was trying so hard to fight back tears—and I'm sure she was too. I don't even know what she said to me next. I told her to let everyone know and that I will be back to work on Monday. She said, "I will and I am praying for you." I said, "Thanks! See you on Monday."

I was nervous about returning to work that Monday. I didn't want any strange looks or sad faces looking at me or anyone feeling sorry me. It wasn't that way at all. Everyone rallied around me and they were all wearing pink breast cancer bracelets to show their support. Everyone let me know that they were all praying for me and to let them know if there was anything they could do for me. I was so grateful for all their love and support.

Shanika Turner

CANCER FAITH

Cancer may come unexpectedly into your life,
Bringing fear, hard times, and great strife.

Families suffer and the end clearly unknown.
Families are stronger than ever and not alone.

Our personalities must stay optimistic,
Feeling better and free will be realistic.

The experience could be a long, hard ride,
Twists and turns in which you have cried.

When you fight and beat it and go on to live,
Don't forget the people who are here to give.

Love and care will forever and always stay.
Cancer will be knocked out of the way.

Your soul is and will be stronger than this;
It can conquer cancer, destroy and dismiss.

Courage and memories are very much needed,
As tiring treatments have faithfully succeeded.

Friendship, family, and faith cannot be suppressed;
They are the loving souls that make you blessed.

When my love-filled Mom became a cancer survivor,
I soon realized that I was an underwater diver.

You dive in but you never know what is there for you,
It could be your worst experience or the very best view.

Michaela Fournier

TESTIMONIES

We're In This Together

Breast cancer is a topic that is often taken lightly. It's not until you have no choice but to take it seriously that we begin to understand the importance of breast cancer awareness. I haven't overlooked the seriousness of breast cancer, but I will say that I'm one who took the subject lightly. I just thought that breast cancer wasn't for me. I soon learned that breast cancer was already a part of me because it touched my family. Here's my story......

My aunt discovered a lump under her arm that was mentioned in casual conversation to other family members. The topic of my aunt having this lump was discussed among family but no one discussed the possibilities of what the lump could be. The lump began to bother her and she was convinced to go to the local Health Department. It was there that the seriousness of this lump surfaced. She was diagnosed with breast cancer that had progressed severely. After receiving chemotherapy, she lost her short battle to breast cancer. The thing I remember the most about her illness is that her personality remained the same. But it's not always a sad story......

During my second experience with breast cancer, I became very concerned. This would be the second member of my family to be diagnosed with breast cancer. Once again, I'm speaking of an aunt, who is now a two time survivor. I can't speak much on the first diagnosis because I found out accidently. I had the pleasure of being there during the second diagnosis. I say pleasure because it did me great favor to be there for her. I can't say I did too much because often all I did was listen. My aunt discovered a lump in her breast that appeared the same way it did with the first diagnosis. After doctor's appointments and further testing she once again received the diagnosis of breast cancer. During this time she would talk to me about what was going on with her and I would just listen. I didn't ask many questions but if she asked a question I would answer. But I focused on listening to her. She would often say "I'm not ready to die" whenever we talked. She carried herself as though she was fine but whenever we talked I realized that she had great concern. When I would leave her sometimes I would cry. I didn't cry because I worried about her losing her battle. I cried because I wasn't there the first time and she needed someone then too, to just listen. I'm proud to say she is now an advocate for breast cancer awareness.

During the time of my aunt's second diagnosis I met a lady who had been recently diagnosed with breast cancer. I went into her room and she began to talk. She told me that all she needed was someone to listen. She didn't want to burden her family because they were afraid. But with me she didn't know me and would never see me again. What this stranger would never know is that she was also helping me.

Constance Jones

In 2001 when I discovered that I had a lump in my right breast. I over looked it for about 4 months. When I finally went for my mammogram, the lump showed up in the X-ray. From there, I went to see a surgical oncologist who recommended that it be removed. I had it removed, and with the grace of God it turned out to be just a cyst. Then it happened again in 2009; this time it was my mother. We went for her annual mammogram, and a week later we get something in the mail stating we need to contact her doctor for a diagnostic mammogram. All that meant was that something abnormal showed up on the mammogram that needed further study. Well, we go back for that and they tell us she needs a biopsy. Well, we go for the biopsy thinking that it's just a cyst, but we weren't so lucky. The results came back right lobular carcinoma in situ (LCIS) breast cancer. The doctors tried to tell us that it was not yet cancer but the very beginning stages and can be removed easily. Guess what, it wasn't that easy. Because my mother had two strokes that affected her right side, the treatments could not be done. So now here comes the bombshell, a modified radical right breast mastectomy. That means she is going to lose her right breast. Before we go through with the surgery we decide to see if I need to be tested for the gene due to my previous history. Well, the doctors decided that based on the family history I was safe. On Sept. 9, 2009, the day of the surgery, we get a phone call at 6:00am saying that the doctor was sick and the surgery would be postponed. So, we had all these nerves and the surgery was canceled. Now here we go again preparing mentally for the surgery and recovery.

That Monday we get the call the surgery will be done on Sept. 18, 2009. We had to be at the hospital at 11:00am; the surgery was scheduled for 1:00pm. We arrive and wait and wait and wait. She is finally taken to surgery at about 5:00pm and remains in recover until 7:50pm; She was taken to her room about 11:00pm. I stayed at the hospital until I had to pick-up my three year old child. Before I left, my mom was asleep and comfortable. The next morning the doctor calls me to tell me that my mom is ready to be released. I couldn't believe that she was being released so soon after major surgery. They insisted that she was stable and doing very well. So I arrive at the hospital to pick her up and get a quick course on what I need to look for and how to empty and measure her drainage. Mom was glad to be in her own bed, but I was afraid that the tube might come out and that she would be in so much pain that it couldn't be managed with the medication they sent home with us. I also thought, "What if her active three year old grandson decides to jump in the bed with his grandmother and accidently hits her in the wrong spot?" Luckily we made it through just fine. Here we are 9 months post surgery and all of her tests are coming back clean and free. We are almost one year cancer free, and claiming in God's name that she will remain cancer free in all the years to come.

Amy Ashe

In December 2007, I never thought I would hear my mom tell me that she was diagnosed with breast cancer. When those words parted her lips, I was in disbelief, heavy hearted, and curious to know why God would put my mom in this situation. I always thought to myself, "God what are you trying to tell my mom?" My mom was a single, strong woman who made sure her family and friends were taken care of. She was 41 years old when she was diagnosed with Ductal Carcinoma in Situ (DCIS) stage 1 breast cancer in her right breast. My mom was committed to always getting her annual mammogram. She was not afraid to examine her body. After constantly checking, she noticed a Hershey piece sized lump in her breast and had it surgically removed. Upon examination, the doctor finally diagnosed her with breast cancer.

During my mom's life transition, there were times when we could not afford to live in the house that we just had moved in two months prior to finding out the news. I was a senior in high school, and could not enjoy my last year due to working part time, doctor's appointments and surgery with my mom. It was tough dealing with a woman who had gone from being independent to dependent. My mom had a bilateral mastectomy with a tram flap reconstruction done and as soon as that was completed, she started chemotherapy. It wiped her out for at least two full days, and left her sick and tired. I hated to see my mom in this situation. My attitude started to change and I felt alone a lot. The mother-daughter relationship we once had flew out the window before my eyes. It hurt me so badly to see my mom so sick and not be able to ease or take away her pain.

My auntie had also been diagnosed with breast cancer before my mom found out about her diagnosis. She died in April 2008, and left behind a husband, two children, and family and friends that cared so much about her. She was only 38 years old. Seeing my favorite aunt die frightened me more because I was wondering if my mom would be next to leave me on earth alone. How would I be able to take care of myself? Who will be there for me when I succeed at anything in life? I wanted my mom to be there for everything I achieved. Now that she has been a survivor for three years, she is there, and I appreciate her more than before. You only have one mother! My mother was a fighter, and breast cancer would not defeat her. Our relationship would not be as strong if we hadn't hit rock bottom and learned what life is really about. After all the tears and thoughts running through my mind, I think out of this journey God wanted my mom to learn how to enjoy her life, and take care of herself just as much as she took care of others. The lesson I think God wanted to show me was to be mindful and appreciative of my mother.

Now that it is 2010, my Aunt Carolyn is now battling this disease. I continue to pray for her always! My Aunt Carolyn is strong, and I think that she will get through this as long as she keeps God first, and has faith that everything will be okay.

To all families and friends of people that battle breast cancer or any type of cancer, support your love ones as they go through this phase, because all the encouragement and prayers help! God answers prayers. He is merciful!

Ciara Crenshaw (Debra Monroe)

Trust in the Lord with all your heart, and lean not on your own understanding. In all your ways acknowledge Him and He shall direct your paths. - Proverbs 3:5, 6

When I was about 11 years old my aunt was battling breast cancer. I remember one night my mother told me to pray for my aunt before I go to bed because she was going to have surgery the next day. I didn't ask any questions. I prayed for her that night. I really didn't know what cancer was then; I just knew that it was something that didn't usually have a good outcome. One June 7, 1989 my aunt passed away from breast cancer. I will never forget it. It was the same night my sister graduated from high school. My mother gave me the news when we got home later that night, but she wanted to wait to tell my sister—she didn't want to spoil her graduation night out with friends—she wanted her to have fun.

Years later when my sister and I were talking about our aunt, my sister told me that after our aunt died, she stopped believing in God. She felt like God did not answer her prayers when she prayed for our aunt when she was sick, so she stopped trusting in Him. She thought that if she prayed for our aunt, she would be ok but God took her from us anyway. I began to think that maybe I didn't pray hard enough for her or didn't pray right. It took a while for my sister to build up her trust in God again.

In May of 2000, my mother was diagnosed with breast cancer. I remember when I heard the news. I said to myself, "Oh no! Not again." All I could think about was all the women in my family that had died of breast cancer. My aunt, my grandmother and most of my mother's aunts had all died from breast cancer when they were in their early 30's. Since my mother was almost fifty, I thought that the family "curse" was over but it wasn't. I was devastated! In my mind my mother was already gone and buried. I had no details of my mother's condition, all I knew was she has cancer. I didn't know how bad it was or if it was caught early. I had to put my trust in the Lord and change my way of thinking. I refused to believe that breast cancer was going to take another woman in my family—especially my mother— she's the strongest woman I know! Strong indeed; my mother is now a 10 year breast cancer survivor. Seven years after my mother was diagnosed with breast cancer, the family "curse" showed its ugly face again. This time I would be the one to face one of my deepest fears.

I trusted in God and I knew that he would give me the strength and courage that I needed to fight this disease and be around to take care of my son and see him grow up. I could not cope with the idea of someone else raising my child. Although I knew he would be in good hands, I knew that I had to beat this for me and my son. I trusted my doctors and did what they told me to do. I took advice, prayed about it and did what I felt was best for me. I knew my surgeon was a Christian man—he always showed it in everything he said or did. He assured me that he could remove the cancerous tumor. I knew that God gave him his talents and that he would use those talents to do everything he could to help me win this fight.

One day I was driving home after leaving a doctor's appointment. I had so much on my mind. All of a sudden my life had changed. I had so many appointments and different doctors to meet. I had so much information to deal with at one time and it was just overwhelming! I screamed out and began to cry! I think this was the point when I accepted the fact that I had breast cancer. The song playing on the radio at the time was *More Than I Can Bear* by Kirk Franklin. As I wiped away my tears, I listened to the words of the song. It is one of my favorite gospel songs and I had heard it so many times before, but this time it was different. I was really listening. *"I've gone through the fire and I've been through the flood. I've been broken into pieces, seen lightning flashing from above, but through it all, I remember that he loves me and he cares, and he'll never put more on me than I can bear."* I truly believe that this song was playing on the radio during that time because it was something that God wanted me to know, and it was definitely something I desperately needed to hear. By the time I got home, my tears had dried up and I was feeling a lot better. That was the day I decided I was not going to cry about it (cancer) anymore! I said to myself, "Today God, right now, I am giving this to you. I know that this is not by battle, but it's yours and I trust with every fiber of my being that you will fight this battle for me." From that moment on, I didn't shed anymore tears or think in a negative way. I gave it to God and I left it alone.

Shanika Turner

Every morning when I wake up, I wonder what the new day will bring. Some days are wonderful and some can be strenuous, especially when I'm reminded of my mother's battle with breast cancer. My mother, Gloria Lawrence, was diagnosed with breast cancer five years ago. Not a day passes that I don't think about the struggles she faced and the way it affected our family. Since she was diagnosed, life for my family has simply never been the same.

If someone asked me to describe my mother, I would say that she's hard-working, very determined, loving, and a miracle worker. My mother has always been the one to hold our family together. Throughout my childhood, she was the bread winner and made it possible for my family to live a comfortable life. My mother joined the military at the age of 18 to help support her family and to become a U.S. citizen. She went through all of this so that she could help relocate her family to the United States. I often compared her to a superhero when I was younger because she never complained, even if she was in pain or having a bad day. Throughout her illness, my mother always made the impossible possible so that my siblings and I were always happy-even if she missed out.

I remember a time during my adolescence when my mother had to visit the doctor on several occasions because of abnormal mammograms. All of the biopsies, however, came back negative. Since my mother has always had a history of abnormal mammograms and the results usually came back negative, I was pretty confident she would always be fine following her annual exam. But I will never forget July 2005. My sister and I were preparing for a trip to Jamaica to visit family and had just left a hair salon. My phone rang and my mother was on the other end. She told me that she had some bad news. Immediately I felt weak which made because I had never heard my mother use the kind of tone she spoke with that day. She proceeded to tell me that she had breast cancer. As soon as I heard those two words "BREAST CANCER," I threw the phone to my sister and ran into the apartment. I cried so hard, grew dizzy and couldn't speak for at least an hour. My sister was so worried about me that she totally disregarded the fact that my mother had just given us the news on her diagnosis.

I felt worthless and useless in that moment because I lived two hours away from my parents. I wanted to be there with my mother while she was seeking comfort because of her life-changing diagnosis. Regardless of the distance, my mother tried comforting us instead of the other way around. My sister and I wanted to cancel the trip to Jamaica, but my parents pleaded with us to proceed with our plans. My sister and I did go, but once in Jamaica we spent the entire week in bed thinking about our mother and prayed daily that she would be healed. When we returned from our trip, we headed straight to our parents' house.

As soon as we arrived, my mother came out to greet us. I will never forget the hug my mother, sister and I shared the first time we united after the news of my mother having breast cancer. After seeing her I felt a little relieved and was able to focus a little more on my daily duties and routine. My mother had to start chemotherapy and radiation treatments the following week, but had a difficult time because the drugs they gave her caused an allergic reaction. She was so nervous and eventually had a slight breakdown. After the doctors added a sedative to the medication, though, she went through chemotherapy sessions with ease.

My mother went through chemotherapy for six months and never missed a day of work, proving her superhero status once again. Yet it was hard for me to see her physical appearance change; her hair fell out, her nails turned a dark bluish black, her skin texture changed and she lost weight. When I would look at her, she seemed so helpless and sad, at least that was my perception, because it was difficult for me to adjust to my mother's physical appearance.

As the months passed my mother's appearance improved, she had more energy and grew active again. The chemotherapy and radiation were a successful, even though she had a rough time in the beginning. My mother's diagnosis and subsequent battle with breast cancer made me gain a new respect for her and it also made my family value her more. She was always the one in the family who made things right and always catered to everyone else's needs before her own. In a strange way I think that being diagnosed with cancer was her way of being catered to and for us to wait on her hand and foot for a change. Before that, she never really had time to herself or time to conduct her own business, because she always put others first.

I often ask myself why my mother had to battle cancer, but I was once told to "Never ask why, just try and make the best of it." Things in life happen in strange ways to random people, but it's up to us to make the best of them. This experience taught me to never take anyone or anything for granted because life isn't promised to any of us.

Crystal Lawrence

Living a Life Worth Dying For

This blog is dedicated to the memory of a relative who recently passed after a brief battle with cancer.

If we are honest with ourselves we would know that all of our lives are terminal. We may not have a timetable or detected disease, but the only way that we do not die, is if we are not born. The days, months, and years between those two events however, hold a lifetime of promise. Whenever I have the opportunity to counsel individuals in the area of personal growth, I start with a simple question. "How do you want your epitaph to read?" This question gives us the opportunity to ponder how we want to be remembered. It draws our focus to the things we are passionate about, and makes us attempt to weave that passion throughout the endeavors in our lives in such a way that people notice. We desire our names to become synonymous with this activity, product, or idea. The next step is to have the person go out and live a life that demands such a statement.

Today as I come to grips with my own mortality, I am challenged and am challenging you to write that epitaph. Make it inclusive of the best that you have to offer. Write it in such a way that you leave all of your gifts on the playing field; you won't need them when you are gone. Once you have finished, hang the statement in a place where you can read it daily. Then go out and live it to reality. Live a life that will make you proud. And when that day does finally come, you will have lived a life that has been worth dying for.

Clarence T. Brown

TESTIMONY
How God Brought Me
Through It All

Being diagnosed with breast cancer at age 44 called my attention to so many things that I "thought" were important or seemed to be at least. With God's comforting arms wrapped around me, I realized that life presents its challenges and God strengthens you like only He can. Drawing from that strength is what makes you feel like going on. It makes you feel as if nothing is impossible with Him. He is the God of a second, third, fourth and many more chances because of His love for us.

March 29, 2005, University Hospital's Dr. Lynn Tucker told me I had breast cancer. I am not sure who cried more, me or her. There were other things said that I simply don't remember, because the only words I heard were "You have breast cancer." The journey to recovery began with those words. With fear and shock running through my thoughts I could only think of my husband, Glynn and my Mommy. How would they be able to handle this? How could I? What was more disconcerting was the fact the malignant *adenomyoepithelioma* was a rare type of breast cancer that only six (6) people in the world ever had at that time. It was in stage two. Dr. Tucker worked diligently to find the answers on how to proceed with treatment. While working on the problem at hand it was discovered that I had a second breast cancer, *infiltrating lobular carcinoma in situ* which had a treatable solution. The treatment for the second cancer happened to cure the first. Truly it was a blessing, but at the time it didn't feel that way. Now I understand completely the blessing in the second diagnosis.

As I asked God for guidance, I needed His miracle in my life to heal my body. What was funny was that I didn't actually "feel" sick. One of the silliest things I would hear people say is "You don't look like you have cancer." I didn't know or understand how you "look" when you have cancer. When I say God gives you what you need to get through, He really knows how to do it! Judi was my angel that God placed directly in my path, and I will forever be grateful for her patience, sense of humor but most of all her kindness. She never gave up on me and that made all the difference in the world to my recovery.

My Mom (Mae Woodard) left her home in North Carolina to come and care for me. What a true blessing it was. She always made sure Glynn and I had meals even though most of the time I didn't have an appetite. Having her here made such a difference. She is on oxygen and has her own health issues, but God saw it not robbery for her to be by my side.

My sister (Tuddie) and my best friend (Vernette) tirelessly traveled back and forth from North Carolina to watch over me during doctor's visits and surgeries. My brother (John) continually prayed for healing. Having so many friends, family, co-workers, church members and sometimes strangers to step in and help with this process gave me so much strength. My sister-in-law (Jean Dixon) spent her vacation in Augusta, GA to care for me and her brother. It meant the world to me. When I think of how God kept moving and working through my life tears fill my eyes, because I know the many people who stepped in did not have to do anything. Thank you Lord for so many blessings. There were plenty more, too many to name but the angels know who they are and continue to be in my life. I am sure I am going to get into trouble for names omitted but understanding is needed. My adopted father (Willie Chiles) walked with me during this journey and his prayers lifted me. With every doctor's visit, every surgery and every treatment, he stood close by my side and with my family. His loving kindness will never be forgotten.

I had the pleasure of having another angel by the name of Dr. Edwin T. Johnson, affectionately known to me as Dr. E.T., watch over me while on the journey. With every call made, email sent and letter written, his knowledge and expertise gave me hope. His book "Breast Cancer Black Woman" provided a wealth of information on breast cancer. Most of all his prayers and inspirational tapes he sent me to get through. He is my sister-in-law's (Eloyse Crenshaw-Jackson) friend and her gift to me was his powerful knowledge and prayers.

This is the fifth year since I was diagnosed, and God's favor has been all over my life. Sometimes when I hear the story of a soldier who has lost the battle, I wonder why God left "me" here. In my heart, I believe God's plan for my life is so much greater than what I ever imagined. My purpose is to help others, to lift them up, encourage those who are in need and give the love back that was given to me. No matter what type of cancer those persons may have, give them all of the God in me and whisper their names in prayer. Every story ends differently but each soldier of any cancer stood brave and fought the good fight. I will always fight with everything inside of me until a cure is found.

Surrounded by family and friends the journey has been rocky at times, but through it all God kept me. My heart is thankful, my soul says yes to Him. Giving up was never an option. It always came down to perseverance and prayer. I would not trade anything for my journey. God has made me stronger, wiser and less likely to become upset, much more tolerant and definitely more appreciative of life, for those things and so much more I say thank you Lord for bringing me through and for giving me so many angels through this journey.

How God Brought Me Through It All

One word—prayer. I have a praying mother and great-grandmother too. All of my family, friends, co-workers and employers where all praying for me; I couldn't or didn't have time to feel sorry for myself. I had to pray for me too. I thank God for surrounding me with a loving support team. I had to remain positive and put God first.

In the beginning, I wondered "Why Now?" I know that things happen for a reason and that it is not up to me to figure out why. God doesn't make mistakes. He chose this for me, and I believe it was a test of my faith, and I passed with flying colors. It's my cancer, I've accepted my cancer, I gave it to God and he healed me. If I had to do it all over again, I wouldn't change a thing. My faith remains constant—the good Lord will always see me through—he will never put more on me than I can bear.

Judith Davis-Crenshaw

STILL STANDING

I'm still standing strong.
Still holding on.
My path is rocky and long,
But I'm still going.

I'm still on this ride.
Partying with friends.
Knowing no pride.
Loving every day with no end.

I'm still wishing on stars,
And shining bright.
Nothing is to far;
When you've got God's light.

I'm still loving life.
Being me.
No drama or strife.
I'm free.

I'm still standing tall.
No one in my way.
I'm making my mistakes and might fall,
But I'm living day to day.

I'm still standing straight.
There's chances I'll fail.
There's no time for hate.

I know love will prevail.

I'm still standing strong.
Happiness is in my heart.
Listening to my own song.
Never falling apart.

Still holding on to the good.
Without fear.
Like I should.
Everything is clear.

I'm still standing.

October 24, 2007

By Amara13

TESTIMONIES

I'M STILL STANDING

As hard as the fight is to beat breast cancer, I'm Still Standing. When I was diagnosed with breast cancer, I never thought about the disease but rather what is going to happen to my children; that's why I immediately chose to become a SURVIVOR. If you have ever received the call that the doctors want to talk to you about your mammogram or they need you to take another one, your heart immediately skips a beat. Your worse fear comes to your mind. The days get longer leading up to that next doctor's visit. Going home after being diagnosed with breast cancer was a scary day. Breast Cancer is a personal journey for me and everyone must decide what SURVIVAL means to them. Going thru the mastectomy that followed was rigorous. You wonder will anyone love you without your breast. How will I date with one breast? Will I live to see my children grow up? Will I live through this? It has been 12 years for me, and I know you can live through it. There are many decisions a woman must make when she is faced with breast cancer. As I participate in many breast cancer walks, I know that there is HOPE. Hope is in the doctors who make the discovery. Hope is in the hands of the surgeon who performs the operation. Hope is in the survivors who walk for themselves. Hope is a PINK RIBBON.

I SURVIVED!!!!!!!!!!!!!!!!

12 year breast cancer survivor, daughter – Raven S. Norris 20 years old a Junior at Augusta State University; Noah M. Cummings 26 years old attending College.

Marilyn Norris

I found my lump in my right breast in April 2003. [This resulted in] Biopsies every year thereafter; results benign until December 2007. Devastating results -- I too have Breast Cancer: DCIS. My sister Marjorie and I were diagnosed approximately five months apart -- with breast cancer! Hearing her tell me those words were devastating. Even more so when I heard that I also have Breast Cancer. Is this really happening? I'm too young for this! I'm only 42! I fell to my knees in disbelief when I received my results and asked GOD "Why?" My physicians picked me up off the floor and comforted me and promised to take good care of me. I was frightened. What was I suppose to do? I had two teenage children still at home to take care of; I had a mortgage to pay and so on. Lord, I ask you to guide me, help me because I surly can't do this alone! All of this devastating information, what am I to do with it?

I did manage to blurt out this information through the tears to my sister Carolyn and my best friend Lisa and made them promise not to tell anyone. I kept this information from the rest of my family, because I didn't want to ruin the Christmas holiday. And I surely couldn't tell Marjorie. Marjorie was still in denial that she had stage four breast cancer. Again, I prayed about when to tell my children and how I needed to tell them. My three children were sobbing in disbelief and scared for me - for us! What I have always known is that "Prayer changes things!" So I asked my Lord and Savior to help me through this Journey and help me overcome and win this battle with Breast cancer. I continued my research on DCIS in order to make decisions on what I was going to do (surgery, reconstruction, and chemotherapy and/or radiation therapy). Based on my research, I decided to have the lumpectomy and Sentinel node biopsy in January 2008, one month later a bi-lateral mastectomy with tram flap (tummy tuck) reconstruction surgery. Three months to recoup before beginning chemotherapy.

We lost our beloved youngest sister Marjorie 37, in April 2008. Anxiety was at its peak! I felt as if I were having a heart attack and unable to sleep days at a time. My coach is gone, she had been there done that. Now it's May 2008 and I start chemotherapy. The feeling of loneliness is overwhelming. My coach is gone, she would have prepared me for what to expect next! I went through six rounds of aggressive chemotherapy because of family history (our step-sister was diagnosed Stage 3 Breast

Cancer in January 2009) that started with the three of us. Before I received my second treatment I was bald. A spray of water from my shower head took a patch of my hair out and down the drain it all went. I screamed, I thought I was prepared but mentally I wasn't. I was warned and also read that I would lose my hair. I was losing my beautiful dark brown shoulder length hair. Lisa my beautician and best friend came over right away and assisted me into her car, and we went to her house. Lisa couldn't shave my head because of the tears in her eyes. So Nakomia, Lisa's husband shaved my head and I shaved his. It might sound like no big deal, but Nakomia never ever goes bald. We took pictures and compared the prettiest head. Of course I had the prettiest bald head. We would go to church, and as soon as I got in the car I would take off my wig. People just looked and stared but that was ok. I would tease my family that I was going to take my wig off in church and put it in the collection plate! LOL! I had to have some humor to get through this! A brisk wind would lift my eyebrows and eyelashes off my face. I quickly learned how to draw eyebrows and wrap a scarf. By my fourth treatment I was really sick and bedbound. Zofran was my best friend. I couldn't eat or swallow because of mouth sores from the tip of my tongue to the end of my trachea. The pain so intense I drooled vs. swallowing. Emergency room here I come again because of dehydration. Unsuccessful IV starts because I'm so dry. Very close to becoming neutropenic. It was during this time I didn't want to be inside of me; No more pain, nausea and vomiting! I wanted to throw in the towel because I didn't think I could live like this any longer. I started losing HOPE! Just as I was starting to feel a little better it was time for another round of chemo. It was at this time I began to question GOD again. What is it that you want me to do with this? Are you going to carry me through this journey you are sending me on? Lord, please don't leave me! Then I heard my grandson Kameron, 11 months old crying at the foot of his bed saying "Nana." When I repositioned myself he was looking at me. I really started crying, then I began to ask GOD to help me and give me the strength to overcome this pain, nausea and vomiting. I realized why I had to fight.

I completed chemo in September 2008. Still weak, I had to go through physical therapy to get my body realigned. I was standing in an upside down L shape, unable to stand erect as a result of four months in the bed. By GOD's grace I'm still standing. I'm back to working full-time and enjoying my family and friends. I've learned to live with it! In the beginning I thought I was served a death sentence, but….. It turned out to be a life sentence. I quickly learned that "Faith Conquers Fear!" It's tough at times; I get fatigued easily but we can get through anything with faith and hope. So, I say to my sister Carolyn (also diagnosed January 2010 with Breast Cancer) to stay strong, keep praying and keep the faith. Many blessings for all those who encouraged me, supported me financially and emotionally, fed me, bathed me and shaved their head for me. This had affected everyone around me. I made new friends along the way who also inspired me to fight, and I HOPE I have inspired someone. And to all women and men, please self exam.

Debrea Monroe

Give God The Glory

A routine examination by my doctor in October 2009 greatly changed life for me and my family (Somebody say, [1]"God is good.") She ordered me to have a baseline mammogram for no particular reason. She just decided that it was time for me to have one. My dear friend played a major part in this life change as well. I wanted to cancel the appointment and stay home because it was raining, and she told me that I better get up and go have it done, since I was already battling other chronic conditions affecting my health. So, I went. During the last week of October, I found out I had cancer in my right breast. Many thoughts ran through my mind with my Stage III diagnosis. I wanted to give up; I wanted to die, and then I remembered how my mom was so strong when any obstacle came her way. I remembered seeing her praying, listening to gospel music and crying, but she kept going, praying, believing and having faith in God. She also continued to raise my girls until she was called home.

---

[1] Psalm 34:8 KJV

I thought, if I didn't try to survive then my kids would be losing a mom all over again. I knew that would not be fair to them. I also had my sister who had taken my mother's role, and I could not put all of that on her. I often thought about how strong my mother was and how she made it through her obstacles, as well as the conversations with my family members, friends and co-workers. I had a few co-workers who provided encouragement by telling me about God's word. That's when I decided to renew my mind (Romans 12:2), and prepare myself to fight this dreadful disease.

In the beginning, I had to undergo a series of tests before beginning treatment. I went back and forth to appointments for me and my children, and of course I still had to work. I experienced anxiety while waiting on the results from all of these tests. While going through all of that, I wanted to give up, because it seemed like too much to bear. Then I saw how God had blessed me. All of my results came back negative; the cancer was just in one localized spot and had not spread. I had a change of heart, got a little stronger and decided to keep on going. By the second chemotherapy (chemo) treatment, I started experiencing side effects. My hair fell out; I felt mortified and wanted to distance myself from everyone. When I saw my oldest daughter break down, I made the decision then to stay strong. It was three days before Christmas, and I was missing my mother. On Christmas day my kids had to clean up after me, and tried to make me eat. I was deeply depressed and just wanted it to end. A soft voice whispered to me, "Keep going; I got you."

I kept going, getting a little stronger. Then I started having excruciating leg pain. I couldn't walk normally because I could not bend my legs or stretch them out. Almost every day I went to the doctor, and they insisted the pain was from the chemotherapy. Finally, one of the doctors decided to run some tests, and he discovered a blood clot. While I was in the hospital thinking about missing work, wondering how I would pay the bills, making sure my girls got to school, and making sure they were mentally ok, I prayed and told God about it. I then made up my mind to just keep going, keep praying, keep believing and keep the faith. I was in low spirits, because I was having side effects from the chemo. I was barely working and now this was happing to me. However, I found out that God outweighs any situation.

I had two co-workers come by and tell me about

God's word, encourage me, and pray with me. This helped me along the way. I was doing pretty well after that except for the sickness from the chemo. March came and the pain in my legs started again. I went to the emergency room because the pain was so unbearable. I was admitted for very low blood pressure and the pain in my leg. After a few tests, I was diagnosed with muscular infraction (my leg had an attack) and dehydration which could have been caused from my diabetes or the chemo. They told me that it would be six months to a year before I would be able to walk normally again, and that I would need to be on crutches for that period of time; but I kept "hopping" along, I kept praying, I kept believing and I kept the faith. Within a month I was walking with 85% normalcy.

Prior to my last two treatments of chemo, my heart function had decreased. I was taken off one of the therapies. I was about to let that get me down, but then I was told in the same session that they couldn't find the lump; the lump had shrunk. After my last chemo treatment, I went back for a visit and still the lump could not be located. I started preparing for my surgery. During my first surgery, they removed six lymph nodes.

They were sent to the pathologist and the results came back negative – no cancer. God is able! I then prepared for my next surgery, the lumpectomy. They removed the tissue where the lump was and sent it to the pathologist as well. It came back NEGATIVE. God is awesome! This is why I kept going, praying, believing and keeping the faith. Even though I came out of one obstacle and faced another, He still brought me out. I AM CANCER FREE!

After all of that, I was hoping to be finished with my physical ailments. However, I found out that I would have to have 6 1/2 weeks of radiation, every day except for the weekend. I broke down when she told me that, but I remembered where I had come from. I knew that with God I would still be going, praying, believing, and keeping the faith, and I was surely going to make it through this situation.

Before all of this, I was working three jobs. While fighting cancer, I was down to one job, and guess what? I survived! The bills got paid, kids did not go hungry, I was not running from one job to another, so I had more time for God, and I got to know Him and the wonderful things He had done and could do. God is great and greatly to be praised. God wants us to know Him. He will have it so that the only thing you can do is get to have that personal relationship with Him. Do it while you can so you won't have to face a dreadful situation. It took cancer for me to slow down. It also took me being in the bed day after day, and night after night, looking at my young daughters taking care of me. At that time, I decided to call on Him first instead of calling on other people. I also realized that people will leave you in your time of need. There were no more invitations to the club or parties, and no more going out to eat, because when you can't keep up with the world they let you go. However, God will forgive you and continue to bless you. It took cancer for me to tell the world that He lives, and all He wants us to do is live for Him, to serve Him, and to be a servant for him.

The American Medical Association (AMA) recommends regular breast screenings beginning at age 40 (I was 38). My doctor though it would be a good idea to do a baseline mammogram a little early. God knows all things. I encourage you to do self breast exams, stay current with your doctor, eat right, live right and try to stay stress free. If you feel something abnormal in your breast, please get it checked. Accept the Lord Jesus as your personal Savior, have that close relationship with Him, because if you keep going, praying, believing and keeping the faith, you will make it. Nobody can love or do you like Jesus. Look to Jesus and not man. Study His word and you will become stronger each day. When the enemy tries to attack you, pray, read the word and speak the word over your life and situation. Friends and family members will leave you. It may be because they don't know how to handle the situation or they just choose not to; do not worry. You continue going, praying, believing, and keeping the faith.

How great is our God! Sing along with me "How great is our God?" All will see the true greatness of our God. His name is the name above all names. He is worthy of all praise. My heart will sing about the greatness of our God.

Surround yourself with positive, equally yoked people. Regardless of the obstacles that you face, with Him you can run through them and emerge better than before.

> *"Don't look at the messenger, Listen to the message"*
>
> Revelation 12:11 says we overcome our enemy be the blood of the Lamb and by the word of our testimony.

COOP - MZ Survivor

One day in August 2001, my family and I were getting ready to leave for a weekend trip to Atlanta. It was very hot, which meant I would be wearing a sleeveless shirt. As I was shaving under my arms, I noticed a lump. It felt odd but I felt fine. So I decided not to tell anyone. The trip went as planned. Monday morning I returned to work and had the nurse, who I worked with take a look at the lump. She asked if the lump caused me any pain. I replied, "No it does not." She then advised me to see my family physician. I made the appointment with my family physician a couple of days later. My family physician assessed the lump and asked me about my caffeine intake. I told her I could not survive without chocolate, coffee, and coke. She then told me that I had a benign cyst caused by the amount of caffeine that I consume. She proceeded to schedule me for a biopsy because the lump was too large for her to remove. This meant that I would have to make an appointment in the cancer clinic. Waiting to talk to an oncologist about a biopsy was very frightening. I think I was most afraid of the atmosphere. Everyone in the clinic had some form of cancer, and I was told I had a caffeine induced cyst. I felt out of place. The oncologist finally came in and viewed the lump. She told me, "It does not look cancerous, and you are only 27, you will be fine." After being reassured, we scheduled my biopsy and I left the office. A week later, the biopsy was performed without any complications. I felt fine, and returned to work on Monday. I went back to the cancer clinic the following week to have the bandage removed. I was fine until I walked into the clinic. For some reason it felt different. I almost felt as though I belonged there. I think God was preparing me for the news I was about to receive. I was placed in a room to see the doctor, but the nurse came in. She asked me if I were alone. I replied, "Yes, I am on my lunch break, is there a problem?" She said, "The doctor is on her way." From that point I can only remember being told, "Tamika, you have breast cancer." After crying, praying, crying, and praying, I decided I could beat this. Please don't get me wrong, there were times I felt like giving up, but the look in my children's eyes would not let me. At the time of my diagnosis, my daughter was 8 years old and my son was 4 years old. I can remember my daughter asking me, "Mommy, will I get breast cancer?" That question triggered the fight in me. My response to her was, "Not if I can help it." I started a fight that I knew I was capable of winning because I was determined not to let my daughter hear the words, you have breast cancer. I started asking my mom about our family history of breast cancer. I was told I had three Aunts who had breast cancer. After researching the type of cancer I had, my family and I sat down with my oncologist to decide on a plan of treatment. I was told my cancer was only stage one. I was also told I could have a lumpectomy with radiation, but the chance of reoccurrence was a possibility. I opted for a mastectomy and breast reconstruction. I had a really strong urge to cut the cancer out completely. I was told my lymph nodes were cancer free, and I was estrogen receptor negative. This all meant that I caught the cancer in its early stage.

Four surgeries and one breast prosthesis later, I am cancer free. I am an advocate for early detection because I can honestly say it saves lives. I urge young women to perform monthly self breast exams. I urge them because, we as women, have to be in charge of our bodies. We have to be advocates. I am reminded everyday that I have to be the voice for early detection. I will walk, talk, run, or do whatever it takes to have a world free of cancer. I want to leave you with this thought - Life is a gift from God, thank Him daily, and know that He does not give you anything that you cannot handle.

Tamika Cook

APPENDIX:

BREAST CANCER RESOURCE MATERIAL

What Is Breast Cancer

Breast Cancer is a disease in which malignant (cancer) cells form from the tissue of the breast. It is considered a heterogeneous disease- different by individual, age group and even the kinds of cells within the tumors themselves. Obviously no one wants to receive this diagnosis, but hearing the word "breast cancer" doesn't always mean the end of the world or your life. It can be the beginning of learning how to fight the fight. Getting and understanding the facts, keeping your trust and faith in God, and praying that we will be able to found a cure.

Breast Cancer Risk Factors

Rest factors for breast cancer include:

- **Age:** Half of all women diagnosed are over age 65.
- **Weight:** Being obese or overweight.
- **Diet & Lifestyle:** Lack of physical activity, a diet high in saturated fat, and alcoholic intake of more than two drinks per day.
- **Menstrual & Reproductive History:** Early menstruation or late menopause, having your first

child at an older age or not having given birth, or taking birth control pills for more than ten years if you are under 35.

- **Family & Personal History:** A family history of breast cancer-particularly a mother, sister, or a personal history of breast cancer of being (non-cancer) can get the breast cancer disease.

- **Medical & Other Factors:** Dense breast tissue (often identified by a mammogram), past radiation therapy to the breast or chest area. A history of hormone treatments-such as estrogen and progesterone, or gene changes-including Breast Cancer 1, Breast Cancer 2, and others.

Breast Self-Exam

Taking a few minutes to do a breast self-exam a minimum of once a month can make a lifetime of difference. Nearly 70% of all breast cancers are found through self-exams, and with early detection the five (5) year survival rate is 98%. If you find a lump, schedule an appointment with your doctor, but don't panic- 8 out of 10 lumps are not cancerous. To have peace of mind, call your doctor whenever you have concerns.

How To Do A Breast Self-Exam

In the Shower

Fingers flat move gently over every part of each breast, Use your right hand to examine the left breast. Check for any lump, hard knot, or thickening. Carefully observe any changes in your breast.

Before a Mirror

Inspect your breast with your arms at your sides. Next, raise your arms high overhead. Look for any changes in the contour of each breast, a swelling, a dimpling of the skin, or changes in the nipple. Then rest you're your palms on your hips and press firmly to flex your chest muscles. Left and right breast will not exactly match- few women's breast do.

Lying Down

Place a pillow under your right shoulder and put your right arm behind your head. With the fingers of your left hand flat, press your right breast gently in small circular motions, moving vertically or in a circular pattern covering the entire breast.

Use light, medium, and firm pressure. Squeeze the nipple: check for discharge and lumps. Repeat these steps for your left breast.

Detection

Early breast cancer usually doesn't cause symptoms. But as the tumor grows, it can change how the breast looks or feels.

Symptoms

Common changes to the breast include:

- A lump or thickening in or near the breast or in the underarm area

- A change in the size or shape of the breast

- Dimpling or puckering in the skin of the breast

- A nipple turned inward into the breast

- Discharge (fluid) from the nipple, especially if it's bloody

- Scaly, red, or swollen skin on the breast, nipple, or (the dark area of skin at the center of the breast).

The skin may have ridges or pitting so that it looks like the skin of an orange.

You should see your health care provider about any symptom that does not go away. Most often, these symptoms are not due to cancer. Another health problem could cause them. If you have any of these symptoms, you should tell your health care provider so that the problems can be diagnosed and treated

Your doctor can check for breast cancer before you have any symptoms. During an office visit, your doctor will ask about your personal and family medical history. You'll have a physical exam. Your doctor may order one or more imaging tests, such as a mammogram.

Doctors recommend that women have regular and mammograms to find breast cancer early. Treatment is more likely to work well when breast cancer is detected early.

You may want to read the NCI booklet **Understanding Breast Changes**. It describes types of breast changes and tests used to find changes.

Clinical Breast Exam

During a clinical breast exam, your health care provider checks your breasts. You may be asked to raise your arms over your head, let them hang by your sides, or press your hands against your hips.

Your health care provider looks for differences in size or shape between your breasts. The skin of your breasts is checked for a rash, dimpling, or other abnormal signs. Your nipples may be squeezed to check for fluid.

Using the pads of the fingers to feel for lumps, your health care provider checks your entire breast, underarm, and collarbone area. A lump is generally the size of a pea before anyone can feel it. The exam is done on one side and then the other. Your health care provider checks the lymph nodes near the breast to see if they are enlarged.

If you have a lump, your health care provider will feel its size, shape, and texture. Your health care provider will also check to see if the lump moves easily. Benign lumps often feel different from cancerous ones. Lumps that are soft, smooth, round, and movable are likely to be benign.

A hard, oddly shaped lump that feels firmly attached within the breast is more likely to be cancer, but further tests are needed to diagnose the problem.

Mammogram

A mammogram is an x-ray picture of tissues inside the breast. Mammograms can often show a breast lump before it can be felt. They also can show a cluster of tiny specks of calcium; these specks are called microcalcifications. Lumps or specks can be from cancer, cells, or other conditions. Further tests are needed to find out if abnormal cells are present.

Before they have symptoms, women should get regular to detect breast cancer early:

- Women in their 40s and older should have mammograms every 1 or 2 years.

- Women who are younger than 40 and have risk factors for breast cancer should ask their health care provider whether to have mammograms and how often to have them.

If the mammogram shows an abnormal area of the breast, your doctor may order clearer, more detailed images of that area. Doctors use to learn more about unusual breast changes, such as a lump, pain, thickening, nipple discharge, or change in breast size or shape. Diagnostic mammograms may focus on a specific area of the breast. They may involve special techniques and more views than screening mammograms.

To learn more about mammograms, you may want to read the NCI fact sheet Mammograms.

Other Imaging Tests

If an abnormal area is found during a clinical breast exam or with a mammogram, the doctor may order other imaging tests:

- **Ultrasound:** A woman with a lump or other breast change may have an ultrasound test. An ultrasound device sends out sound waves that people can't hear. The sound waves bounce off breast tissues. A computer uses the echoes to create a picture. The picture may show whether a lump is solid, filled with fluid (a), or a mixture of both. Cysts usually are not cancer. But a solid lump may be cancer.

- **MRI:** MRI uses a powerful magnet linked to a computer. It makes detailed pictures of breast tissue. These pictures can show the difference between normal and diseased tissue.

Biopsy

A biopsy is the removal of tissue to look for cancer cells. A biopsy is the only way to tell for sure if cancer is present.

You may need to have a biopsy if an abnormal area is found. An abnormal area may be felt during a clinical breast exam but not seen on a mammogram. Or an abnormal area could be seen on a mammogram but not be felt during a clinical breast exam. In this case, doctors can use imaging procedures (such as a mammogram, an ultrasound, or MRI) to help see the area and remove tissue.

Your doctor may refer you to a surgeon or breast disease specialist for a biopsy. The surgeon or doctor will remove fluid or tissue from your breast in one of several ways:

- **Fine-needle aspiration biopsy:** Your doctor uses a thin needle to remove cells or fluid from a breast lump.

- **Core biopsy:** Your doctor uses a wide needle to remove a sample of breast tissue.

- **Skin biopsy:** If there are skins changes on your breast, your doctor may take a small sample of skin.

- **Surgical biopsy:** Your surgeon removes a sample of tissue.

  o An incisional biopsy takes a part of the lump or abnormal area.

  o An excisional biopsy takes the entire lump or abnormal area.

A pathologist will check the tissue or fluid removed from your breast for cancer cells. If cancer cells are found, the pathologist can tell what kind of cancer it is. The most common type of breast cancer is ductal carcinoma. It begins in the cells that line the breast ducts. Lobular carcinoma is another type. It begins in the lobules of the breast.

You may want to ask your doctor these questions before having a biopsy:

- What kind of biopsy will I have? Why?

- How long will it take? Will I be awake? Will it hurt? Will I have? What kind?

- Are there any risks? What are the chances of infection or bleeding after the biopsy?

- Will I have a scar?

Lab Tests with Breast Tissue

If you are diagnosed with breast cancer, your doctor may order special lab tests on the breast tissue that was removed:

- **Hormone receptor tests:** Some breast tumors need hormones to grow. These tumors have receptors for the hormones estrogen, progesterone, or both. If the hormone receptor tests show that the breast tumor has these receptors, then hormone therapy is most often recommended as a treatment option. See the Hormone Therapy section.

- **HER2/neu test:** HER2/neu protein is found on some types of cancer cells. This test shows whether the tissue either has too much HER2/neu protein or too many copies of its gene. If the breast tumor has too much HER2/neu, then targeted therapy may be a treatment option. See the Targeted Therapy section.

It may take several weeks to get the results of these tests. The test results help your doctor decide which cancer treatments may be options for you.

Breast Cancer in Men

Statistics Regarding Men and Breast Cancer

Breast cancer in men is rare—less than 1 percent of all breast carcinomas occur in men. Consider the latest statistics available from the American Cancer Society (ACS):

The ACS estimates that in 2009, approximately 1,910 new cases of invasive breast cancer were diagnosed among men in the United States. Breast cancer is about 100 times more common among women. The average age at diagnosis is 67, although men of all ages can be affected with the disease.

What are risk factors for breast cancer in men?

Risk factors may include:

- Radiation Exposure
- Estrogen administration
- Diseases associated with hyperestrogenism, such as cirrhosis or Klinefelter's syndrome

Also, there are definite familial tendencies for developing breast cancer:

- An increased incidence is seen in men who have a number of female relatives with breast cancer.

- An increased risk of male breast cancer has been reported in families in which a BRCA2 gene mutation has been identified.

What is the most common type of breast cancer in men?

Infiltrating ductal cancer is the most common tumor type, but intraductal cancer, inflammatory carcinoma, and Paget's disease of the nipple have been seen as well. Lobular carcinoma in situ is very rare in men.

What are the symptoms of breast cancer in men?

The following are the most common symptoms of breast cancer in men. However, each individual may experience symptoms differently. Symptoms may include:

- Breast lumps

- Nipple inversion

- Nipple discharge (sometimes bloody)

- A pain or pulling sensation in the breast

The symptoms of breast cancer may resemble other medical conditions or problems. Always consult your physician for a diagnosis.

What are the similarities to breast cancer in women?

Lymph node involvement and the hematogenous pattern of spread (through blood) are similar to those found in female breast cancer. The staging system for male breast cancer is identical to the staging system for female breast cancer. Prognostic factors that have been evaluated include the size of lesion and the presence or absence of lymph node involvement, both of which correlate well with prognosis.

Overall survival rates are similar to that of women with breast cancer. The impression that male breast cancer has a worse prognosis may stem from the tendency toward diagnosis at a later stage.

Treatment for Men with Breast Cancer

Specific treatment for male breast cancer will be determined by your physician based on:

- Your age, overall health, and medical history

- Extent of the disease

- Your tolerance for specific medications, procedures, or therapies

- Expectations for the course of the disease

- Your opinion or preference

The primary standard treatment is a modified radical mastectomy because breast- conserving therapy is not an option due to the lack of glandular breast tissue in men. Other treatment may include:

- **Radiation therapy** - Radiation therapy is a process that precisely sends high levels of radiation directly to the cancer cells. Radiation done after surgery can kill cancer cells that may not be seen during surgery. Radiation may also be done:

  o Before surgery to shrink the tumor.

  o In combination with chemotherapy.

o As a palliative treatment (therapy that relieves symptoms, such as pain, but does not alter the course of the disease).

Radiation therapy is usually delivered by external beam radiation. External radiation (also called external beam therapy) is a treatment that precisely sends high levels of radiation directly to the cancer cells. The machine is controlled by the radiation therapist. Since radiation is used to kill cancer cells and to shrink tumors, special shields may be used to protect the tissue surrounding the treatment area. Radiation treatments are painless and usually last a few minutes.

- **Chemotherapy** - Chemotherapy is the use of anticancer drugs to treat cancerous cells. In most cases, chemotherapy works by interfering with the cancer cell's ability to grow or reproduce. Different groups of drugs work in different ways to fight cancer cells. The oncologist will recommend a treatment plan for each individual.

- **Hormone therapy** - In some cases, hormones can kill cancer cells, slow the growth of cancer cells, or stop cancer cells from growing. Hormone therapy as a cancer treatment involves taking substances to interfere with the activity of hormones or to stop the production of hormones.

Before you begin hormone therapy, your physician may recommend a hormone receptor test. This lab test is performed on a tissue sample to determine if estrogen and progesterone receptors are present. A hormone receptor test can help to predict whether cancer cells are sensitive to hormones. Tamoxifen is the standard endocrine treatment for men with hormone-sensitive disease. However, more recent studies have suggested a benefit to aromatase inhibitors as well, which are a class of drug that are now routinely used in women with breast cancer.

The hormone estrogen is present in men, as well as in women. Estrogen can increase the growth of breast cancer cells in some men. Hormone therapy may be recommended for men whose breast cancers test positive for estrogen receptors. Antiestrogens, such as tamoxifen, are most often used in hormone therapy of breast cancer in both men and women.

- **Adjuvant therapy** - Radiation therapy, chemotherapy, or hormone therapy are given after surgery for the removal of cancer as a safety factor to kill any cancer cells that cannot be seen. Adjuvant therapy may be considered on the same basis as it is for a woman with breast cancer because there is no evidence that the prognosis is different between men and women.

This content was last modified on May 18, 2007.

STAGING

Stage 0—Carcinoma in situ

In stage zero breast cancer, atypical cells have not spread outside of the ducts or lobules, the milk producing organs, into the surrounding breast tissue. Referred to as carcinoma in situ, it is classified in two types:

- Ductal Carcinoma In Situ (DCIS)— very early cancer that is highly treatable and survivable. If left untreated or undetected, it can spread into the surrounding breast tissue.

- Lobular Carcinoma In Situ (LCIS)—not a cancer but an indicator that identifies a woman as having an increased risk of developing breast cancer.

Stage I—Early stage invasive breast cancer

In stage 1 breast cancer, the cancer is no larger than two centimeters (approximately an inch) and has not spread to surrounding lymph nodes or outside the breast.

Stage II

Stage 2 breast cancer is divided into two categories according to the size of the tumor and whether or not it has spread to the lymph nodes:

- Stage II A Breast Cancer—the tumor is less than two centimeters(approximately an inch) and has spread up to three auxiliary underarm lymph nodes. Or, the tumor has grown bigger than two centimeters, but no larger than five centimeters (approximately two inches) and has not spread to surrounding lymph nodes.

- Stage II B Breast Cancer— the tumor has grown to between two and five centimeters (approximately one to two inches) and has spread to up to three auxiliary underarm lymph nodes. Or, the tumor is larger than five centimeters, but has not spread to the surrounding lymph nodes.

Stage III

Stage 3 breast cancer is also divided in to two categories:

- Stage III-A Breast Cancer—the tumor is larger than two centimeters but smaller than five centimeters (approximately one to two inches) and has spread to up to nine auxiliary underarm lymph nodes.

- Stage III-B Breast Cancer— the cancer has spread to tissues near the breast including the skin, chest wall, ribs, muscles, or lymph nodes in the chest wall or above the collarbone.

Treatment Choices by Stage

Your treatment options depend on the stage of your disease and these factors:

- The size of the tumor in relation to the size of your breast

- The results of lab tests (such as whether the breast cancer cells need hormones to grow)

- Whether you have gone through menopause

- Your general health

Below are brief descriptions of common treatments for each stage. Other treatments may be appropriate for some women. Research studies (clinical trials) can be an option at all stages of breast cancer.

Stage 0 (DCIS)

Most women with DCIS have breast-sparing surgery followed by radiation therapy. Some women instead choose to have a total mastectomy. Women with DCIS may receive tamoxifen to reduce the risk of developing invasive breast cancer.

Stages I, II, III-A, and some III-C

Women with Stage I, II, IIIA, or operable IIIC breast cancer may have a combination of treatments. (Operable means the cancer can be treated with surgery.)

Some may have breast-sparing surgery followed by radiation therapy to the breast. This choice is common for women with Stage I or II breast cancer. Others decide to have a mastectomy.

With either approach, women (especially those with Stage II or IIIA breast cancer) often have lymph nodes under the arm removed.

Whether or not radiation therapy is used after mastectomy depends on the extent of the cancer. If cancer cells are found in 1 to 3 lymph nodes under the arm or if the tumor in the breast is large, the doctor sometimes suggests radiation therapy after mastectomy. If cancer cells are found in more than 3 lymph nodes under the arm, the doctor usually will suggest radiation therapy after mastectomy.

The choice between breast-sparing surgery (followed by radiation therapy) and mastectomy depends on many factors:

- The size, location, and stage of the tumor

- The size of the woman's breast
- Certain features of the cancer
- How the woman feels about how surgery will change her breast
- How the woman feels about radiation therapy
- The woman's ability to travel to a radiation treatment center

You may want to read the NCI booklet <u>Surgery Choices for Women with Early-Stage Breast Cancer</u>.

Some women have chemotherapy before surgery. This is called neoadjuvant therapy (treatment before the main treatment). Chemotherapy before surgery may shrink a large tumor so that breast-sparing surgery is possible. Women with large Stage II or IIIA breast tumors often choose this treatment.

After surgery, many women receive adjuvant therapy. Adjuvant therapy is treatment given after the main treatment to lower the chance of breast cancer returning. Radiation treatment is local therapy that can kill any remaining cancer cells in and near the breast. Women may also have hormone therapy, chemotherapy, targeted therapy, or a combination. These systemic therapies can destroy cancer cells that remain anywhere in the body.

They can prevent or delay the cancer from coming back in the breast or elsewhere.

You may want to read the NCI fact sheet <u>Adjuvant and Neoadjuvant Therapy for Breast Cancer</u>.

Stage III-B and some Stage III-C

Women with Stage IIIB (including inflammatory breast cancer) or inoperable Stage IIIC breast cancer have chemotherapy first, and then may be offered other treatments. (Inoperable means the cancer can't be treated with surgery without first shrinking the tumor.) They may also have targeted therapy.

If the chemotherapy or targeted therapy shrinks the tumor, then surgery may be possible:

- **Mastectomy:** The surgeon removes the breast. In most cases, the lymph nodes under the arm are removed. After surgery, a woman may receive radiation therapy to the chest and underarm area.

- **Breast-sparing surgery:** In rare cases, the surgeon removes the cancer but not the breast. The lymph nodes under the arm are usually removed. After surgery, a woman may receive radiation therapy to the breast and underarm area.

After surgery, the doctor will likely recommend chemotherapy, targeted therapy, hormone therapy, or a combination. This therapy may help prevent the disease from coming back in the breast or elsewhere.

Stage IV and Recurrent

Women with recurrent breast cancer will be treated based on where the cancer returned. If the cancer returned in the chest area, the doctor may suggest surgery, radiation therapy, chemotherapy, hormone therapy, or a combination.

Women with Stage IV breast cancer or recurrent cancer that has spread to the bones, liver, or other areas usually have hormone therapy, chemotherapy, targeted therapy, or a combination. Radiation therapy may be used to control tumors in certain parts of the body. These treatments are not likely to cure the disease, but they may help a woman live longer.

Many women have supportive care along with anticancer treatments. Anticancer treatments are given to slow the progress of the disease. Supportive care helps manage pain, other symptoms of cancer, or the side effects of treatment (such as nausea). This care can help a woman feel better physically and emotionally. Supportive care does not aim to extend life. Some women with advanced cancer decide to have only supportive care.

Material on this page courtesy of The National Cancer Institute

Internet Resources

Facing Our Risk of Cancer Empowered (FORCE) -
Information for people at higher risk of breast cancer
(http://www.facingourrisk.org)

National Cancer Institute – Breast Cancer Risk
Assessment tool
(http://bcra.nci.nih.gov/brc/q1.htm)

<u>Early Detection and Screening</u>

*National Breast and Cervical Cancer Early Detection
Program* - Information on free or low-cost
mammograms (http://cdc.gov/cancer/nbccedp)

<u>Diagnosis</u>

Inflammatory Breast Cancer Research Foundation -
Information on inflammatory breast cancer diagnosis and
care (http://www.ibcresearch.org)

National Cancer Institute (NCI) - Information on
different types of breast cancers as well as other types of
cancer that can occur in the breast, such as phyllodes
tumor (http://www.cancer.gov)

Treatment Clinical Trial Information

CancerConsultants.com - Free and confidential clinical trial matching and referral services (http://www.cancerconsultants.com)

Getting good Care

American Cancer Society - Information on care for people living with cancer (http://www.cancer.org)

National Cancer Institute (NCI) - Information on care for people living with cancer (http://cancer.gov)

American Society of Clincial Oncology (ASCO) (http://www.cancer.net)

After Treatment

Fertile Hope - Provides financial aid to women with breast cancer whose insurance will not cover fertility treatment (http://www.fertilehope.org)

Association of Community Cancer Centers - Find the publication " Cancer Treatments Your Insurance Should Cover"
(http://www.acc-cancer.org)

Medicaid - Find a state's Medicaid toll-free hotline
(http://cms.hhs.gov/medicaid)

Financing Issues – Medical Assistance

Cancer Care - Financial assistance for transportation to and from treatment, Childcare when a parent is having tests or treatment
(http://www.cancercare.org)

Social Support

American Cancer Society – Cancer Survivors Network: Online community for cancer survivors and caregivers
(http://www.acscsn.org)

American Cancer Society – Reach to Recovery
Provides in – person and telephone support for people living with cancer.
(http://www.cancer.org)

Living Beyond Breast Cancer - Information on breast cancer support and care
(http://www.lbbc.org)

Men Against Breast Cancer - Provides services to help me be good caregivers of women with breast cancer
(http://menagainstbreastcancer.org)

The Wellness Community - Provides support to people living with cancer and their families
(http://www.thewellnesscommunity.org)